Red

Moira Anderson

www.raintreepublishers.co.uk

Visit our website to find out more information about **Raintree** books.

To order:
☎ Phone 44 (0) 1865 888112
🖹 Send a fax to 44 (0) 1865 314091
💻 Visit the Raintree Bookshop at **www.raintreepublishers.co.uk** to browse our catalogue and order online.

First published 2005 by Heinemann Library
a division of Harcourt Education Australia,
18–22 Salmon Street, Port Melbourne Victoria 3207
Australia (a division of Reed International Books Australia
Pty Ltd, ABN 70 001 002 357).
Visit the Heinemann Library website
www.heinemannlibrary.com.au

Published in Great Britain by Heinemann Library,
Halley Court, Jordan Hill, Oxford OX2 8EJ,
part of Harcourt Education
www.heinemann.co.uk/library

ℛ A Reed Elsevier company

© Reed International Books Australia Pty Ltd 2005

09 08 07 06 05
10 9 8 7 6 5 4 3 2 1

Editorial: Moira Anderson, Carmel Heron
Design: Sue Emerson (HL-US), Marta White
Photo research: Jes Senbergs, Wendy Duncan
Production: Tracey Jarrett

Typeset in 26/32 pt Infant Gill Regular
Film separations by Print + Publish, Port Melbourne
Printed and bound in China by
South China Printing Company Ltd.

The paper used to print this book comes from sustainable
resources.

**National Library of Australia
Cataloguing-in-Publication data:**

Anderson, Moira (Moira Helen).
    Red.

    Includes index.
    For lower primary school students.
    ISBN 1 74070 289 1.

    1. Colors – Juvenile literature. 2. Red – Juvenile
    literature. I. Title. (Series : Read and learn).
    (Series : Finding colours).

535.6

Acknowledgements
The publisher would like to thank the following for
permission to reproduce photographs: Rob Cruse
Photography: pp. **6, 8, 10, 11**; Corbis: pp. **22, 24**; Getty
Images: p. **16**; Getty Images/PhotoDisc: p. **15**, /National
Geographic/George Grall: pp. **20, 23**; PhotoDisc, pp. **4,
5, 7, 9, 12, 13, 14, 18, 19, 20, 21, 23** (all except frog
feet); photolibrary.com/Plainpicture: p. **17**.

Front cover photograph permission of Tudor
Photography, back cover photographs permission of
Getty Images/National Geographic/George Grall (frog)
and PhotoDisc (grapes).

Every attempt has been made to trace and acknowledge
copyright. Where an attempt has been unsuccessful, the
publisher would be pleased to hear from the copyright
owner so any omission or error can be rectified.

Contents

Some words are shown in bold, **like this**.
You can find them in the glossary on page 23.

What is red?

Red is a colour.

What different colours can you see in this picture?

The colour red is all around.

What do you do with these
red things?

What red things can I eat?

Strawberries are good to eat.

When they are red, we can pick and eat them.

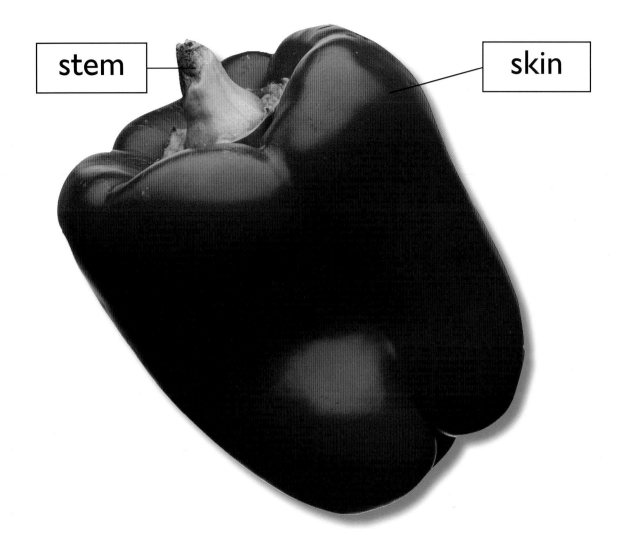

stem

skin

Some peppers are red.

They have red **skin** and a green **stem**.

What red clothes can I wear?

This shirt is made of red **cotton**.

Cotton keeps you cool.

These red mittens are made of **wool**.

Wool keeps your hands warm.

What is red on buildings?

Some buildings are made of red bricks.

Bricks are hard and strong.

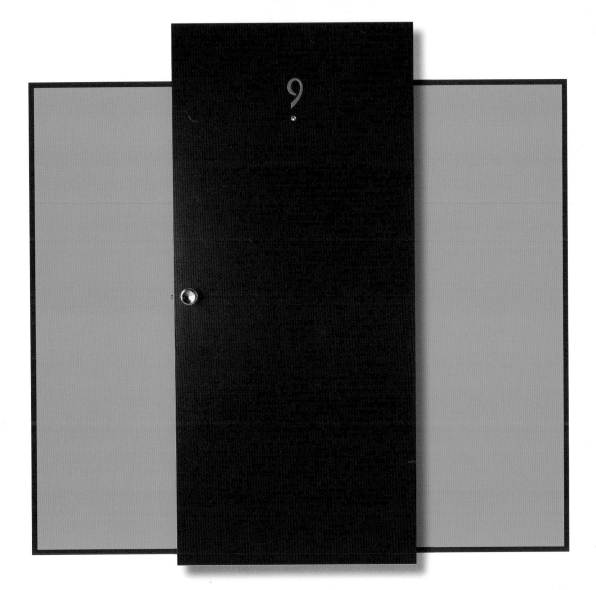

This front door is red.

It is made of wood and painted red.

What is red at home?

handle grips

seat

This tricycle is red.

It has a red seat and handle grips.

This mug is red.

It keeps the cocoa hot.

Can I find red things in a city?

These traffic lights are sometimes red.

When the light is red, traffic must stop.

This fire engine is red.

It is used to fight fires.

Can I find red things in a forest?

Red **berries** grow in a forest.

They are easy to see in the snow.

The **leaves** of this tree are red.

Some leaves turn red in autumn.

Are there red animals?

Red animals live in gardens.

Ladybirds are red insects.

Red animals live in the sea.

This starfish is red and yellow.

How do people celebrate with red?

People **celebrate** Chinese New Year with lots of red.

They put up red lanterns.

People celebrate with fireworks.

Red fireworks look good in the night sky.

Quiz

What red things can you see?

Look for the answers on page 24.

Glossary

berries
small, round, juicy fruit

celebrate
do something special to show a day
or event is important

cotton
material made from the cotton plant;
used to make clothes

leaves
flat parts of a plant that grow from
the stem or a branch

skin
the outer layer of vegetables or
fruit

stem
the centre part of a plant

wool
thread made from soft hair of sheep;
used to make clothes

Index

Answers to the quiz on page 22

paint   smock

table

chairs

Notes to parents and teachers

Reading non-fiction texts for information is an important part of a child's literacy development. Readers can be encouraged to ask simple questions and then use the text to find the answers. Each chapter in this book begins with a question. Read the questions together. Look at the pictures. Talk about what the answer might be. Then read the text to find out if your predictions were correct. To develop readers' enquiry skills, encourage them to think of other questions they might ask about the topic. Discuss where you could find the answers. Assist children in using the contents page, picture glossary and index to practise research skills and new vocabulary.

Titles in the **Finding Colours** series include:

ISBN   1 74070 287 5

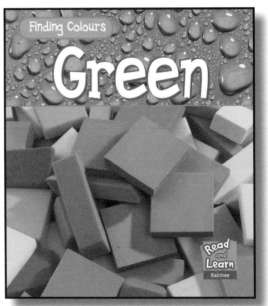

ISBN   1 74070 288 3

ISBN   1 74070 289 1

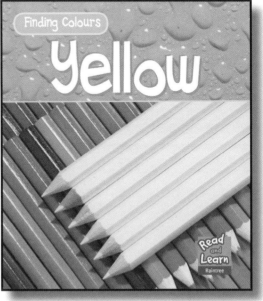

ISBN   1 74070 290 5

Find out about the other titles in this series on our website www.raintreepublishers.co.uk